Simply Cut Out & Use

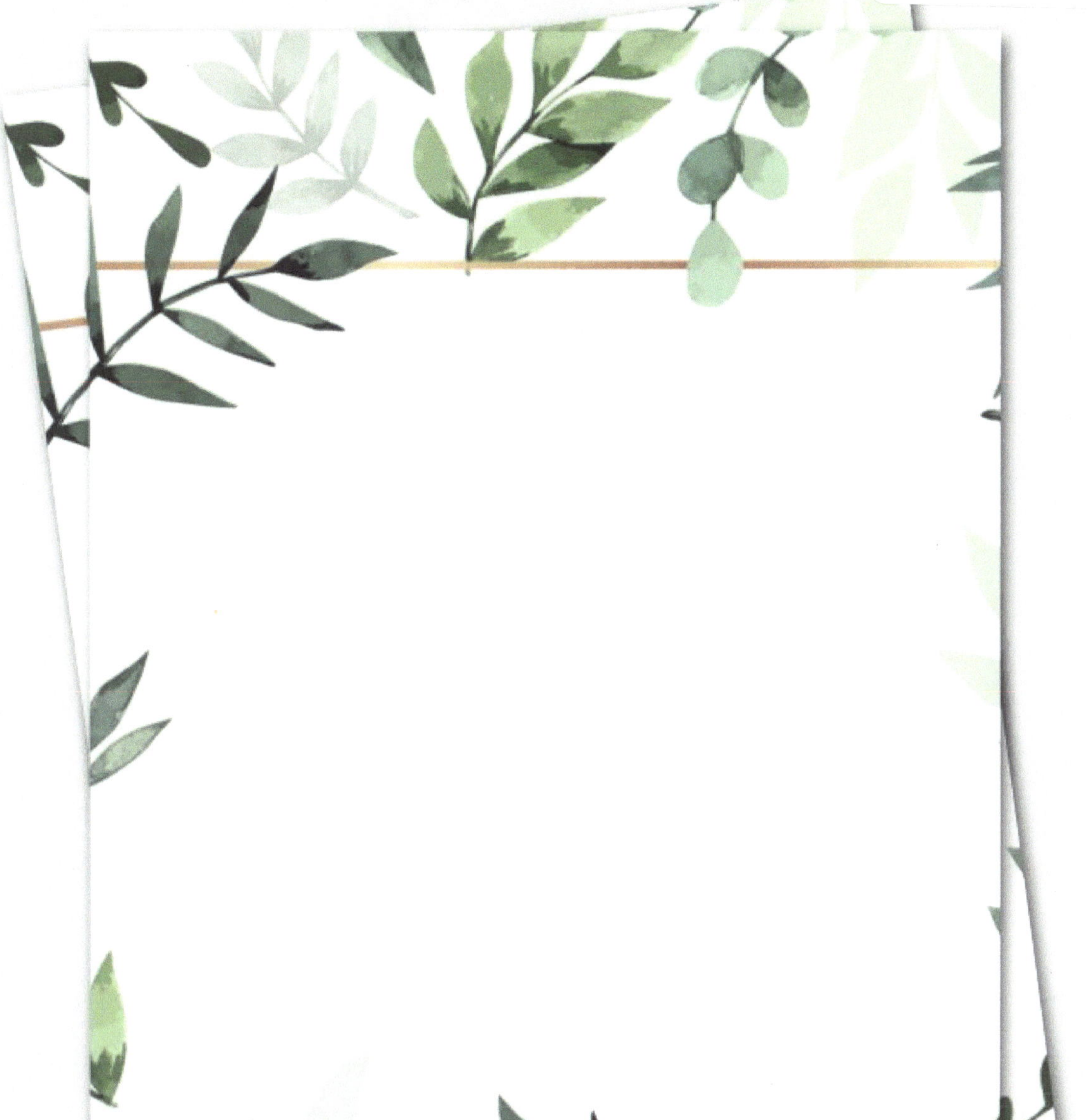

Floral Green Frame

STATIONERY PAPER

25 SHEETS | 5.5" x 8.5" | Half-Letter Size Paper

Simply Cut Out & Use

Simply Cut Out & Use

Simply Cut Out & Use

Simply Cut Out & Use

Simply Cut Out & Use

Simply Cut Out & Use

Simply Cut Out & Use

Simply Cut Out & Use

Simply Cut Out & Use

Simply Cut Out & Use

Simply Cut Out & Use

Simply Cut Out & Use

Simply Cut Out & Use

Simply Cut Out & Use

Simply Cut Out & Use

Simply Cut Out & Use

Simply Cut Out & Use

Simply Cut Out & Use

Simply Cut Out & Use

www.ingramcontent.com/pod-product-compliance
Lightning Source LLC
Chambersburg PA
CBHW042118030726
47599CB00002B/263